School

ILLUSTRATED BY JAN LEWIS

It's hard getting dressed in a hurry!

Where are my shoes?   Are we going to be late?

Would you like juice or milk in your lunch box?

Please will you cut up my apple? Thank you!

There are lots of children here! Are they all new?

Who will help me find my classroom?

If you're worried, just ask a teacher.

Goodbye! Have a lovely day! See you later!

I have the cat peg. I'll hang my bag here.

What have you lost? We'll ask the teacher.

Come with me, we'll find your seat. It's over here.

What are you doing? Can I do some drawing?

How many more blocks do we need? Who knows?

Let's count. Can you add the numbers together?

What fruit do you like best? I like apples!

What drink have you got in your bottle?

It's really noisy out here! You'll get used to it.

Come on, try and catch me! I can run fast!

Clip, clop! Look at me! 8, 9, 10 steps now! Careful!

I can go really fast down this slide! Who's next?

Play the instruments while I clap. Keep in time!

Now, let's sing as loud as we can! That's great!

Try to write slowly and carefully. Well done!

What sound does this letter make? Can you say it?

Oh no! I've spilt some of my lunch! I'll help clear up.

Who has sandwiches? I've got cheese in mine.

Come over here and sit at our table. There's space.

This is delicious! I never have this at home!

Who's in there? I'm finished! It's your turn next.

Wash your hands after using the toilet.

You've got the wrong shoe. I'm sure that's mine!

It fits me! We must have the same size feet!

I love balancing! Now jump off the end! Whee!

Now, can you land in the middle of the hoop?

I'll throw the bean bag! Can you catch it?

Hold out your hands. Watch it carefully. Good try!

How many different shells can you count?

Look! I found a hermit crab peeping out of its shell.

Can you find a starfish? A sea urchin? Any seaweed?

Has anyone been on holiday to the beach?

Does anyone know this book?

What noise do you think the elephant would make?